Pergamano®

Occasions and Celebrations

PAT HOSKING

Pergamano® is the brand name under which books and materials for the creative hobby Parchment Craft are marketed.

ISBN 90-80456-08-X
NUR 475

Photography: Ferry Herrebrugh, Amstelveen, The Netherlands
Cover: Artnic BV, Deventer, The Netherlands
Typesetting: Artnic BV, Deventer, The Netherlands
Printing: Thieme Deventer, Deventer, The Netherlands

CONTENTS

Forword

You have before you Pat Hosking's third book. Once again she has successfully put together a book with unique designs that are so distinctive for her style. I have come to know Pat as a very enthusiastic teacher and I have noticed that, like no one else she is able to pass over this enthusiasm for parchment craft to other people. When this book went into production Pat travelled around the world to demonstrate and teach in Japan, Australia, New Zealand, the Figi Islands and Canada. She is definitely not lacking enthusiasm for parchment craft and I am glad that she shares her passion with so many people worldwide.

"Pat, along this way I would like to thank you for your contribution to spreading this beautiful craft. Thanks to your dedication many people have started to practise the art of parchment craft and others will continue to practise it for years because you have inspired them with new possibilities."

Finally, I would like to congratulate you with the publication of "Occasions and Celebrations" and I am sure that these designs will appeal to people worldwide.

Martha Ospina
Author and president of I.P.C.A.

Introduction

I dedicate this book to my grandchildren, to encourage them and the readers to explore their own creativity. I have no formal art training and had done no art work since school days (when I loved the subject). Until I came across Pergamano Parchment Craft purely by chance. I qualified as one of the first teachers in the UK under Martha's training and quickly realized this was the craft for me.

Acknowledgements
Sincere thanks to many parchment craft enthusiasts from around the world who have encouraged me to write my third book. Your kind comments, requests and interest in my ideas are much appreciated. Many thanks also to my daughter Sarah for assistance with computing, to my husband and family for their enthusiasm and support.

Pat Hosking

Working descriptions

1 Daisies

General
The card is made of regular parchment paper. Two inserts were used: one is made of Parchment Vellum silver (art.no. 1611) and the other one (in shape of a square) is made of regular parchment paper.

Tracing
Tinta leafgreen (10T): leaves. Tinta white (01T): flowers, buds, straight lines, outline of front of card.

Painting
Tinta leafgreen (10T) and Tinta yellow (16T) mixed: leaves. Tinta red (03T) and Tinta fuchsia (20T) mixed (well watered down): tips of the petals and buds.

Perforating (shallow)
With perforating tool Semi Square according to pattern. With Easy-Grid regular mesh and perforating tool Arrow according to pattern A.

Embossing
Small leaves, petals, straight lines, between Semi Square perforations, outline of card and a second wavy line just inside the outline of card. With embossing tool Star according to pattern. With embossing tool Hockey Stick: large leaves.

Perforating (deep)
With perforating tool Semi Square again according to pattern. With perforating tool Arrow (on cutting mat): enlarge the central holes in Semi Square perforations.

Finishing off
Perforate with 2-needle tool along the front of the card and cut out along these perforations. Fold the card. Attach the insert inside the card and cut the back of the card and the insert off straight. Attach the square shaped insert, on which to write on (see tip on pattern Easy Lace Card with Flowers), inside the back of the card.

2 Get Well Soon

General
The card is made of regular parchment paper and the insert of Rainbow parchment paper (art.no. 1483).

Tracing
Tinta Pearl blue (02TP) and Tinta Pearl yellow (16TP) mixed: leaves, stems. Tinta Pearl white (01TP) + Tinta Pearl yellow (16TP) + Tinta Pearl sepia (12TP) + Tinta Pearl red (03TP) + Tinta Pearl blue (02TP): flowers, flower centres according to example. Tinta Pearl white (01TP): outline of card.

Pattern 1

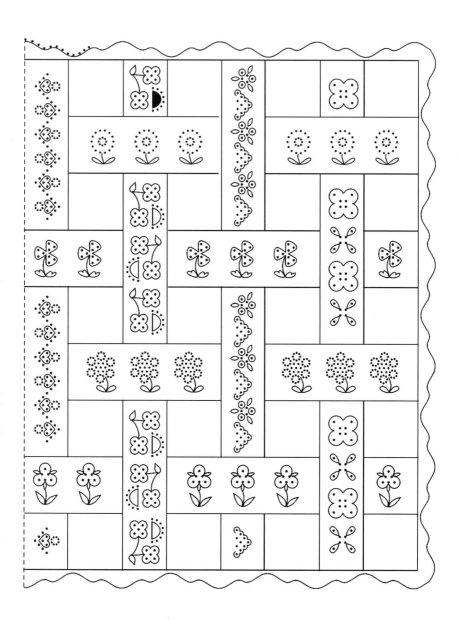

Pattern 2

8

Painting

Tinta leafgreen (10T): leaves.

Perforating (shallow)

With 3-, 5-needle tools and perforating tools Flower, Four-in-Four, Semi Square, Semi Circle according to pattern. With Easy-Grid fine mesh and perforating tool Diamond along inside of the squares.

Embossing

Leaves, straight lines, outline of card and between Four-in-Four, Semi Square, Semi Circle perforations. With embossing tool Star according to pattern. Emboss on front of card: along the inside of the outline of card in "feather drawing" movement.

Perforating (deep)

With 3-, 5-needle tools (twist left/right) again according to pattern. With perforating tools Flower, Four-in-Four, Semi Square, Semi Circle again according to pattern.

Finishing off

Fold the card and perforate along the outline of the card with the perforating tool 2-Split. Cut or tear out the card alng these perforations. Attach the insert with double sided tape inside the card. Add a text sticker.

3 Green Bookmark

General

The bookmark is made of regular parchment paper. Other material: gold ribbon (10cm long, 3mm wide).

Tracing

Tinta white (01T): curved lines. Tinta leafgreen (10T): leaves, stems, outline of bookmark. Tinta orange (06T): flowers. Tinta gold (22T): leaf shapes between flowers, between perforations.

Painting

Tinta leafgreen (10T): leaves. Tinta orange (06T) and Tinta Pearl red (03TP) mixed: flowers.

Perforating

With 1-needle tool according to pattern.

Embossing

Along the outside of the outline of bookmark, curved lines, between gold leafshapes, flowers, leaves and between 1-needle perforations. With embossing tool Star according to pattern.

Pattern 3

Finishing off
Perforate along the outline of the
bookmark with the 2-needle tool and
cut out along these perforations.
Make a hole as indicated. Thread the
ribbon through the hole and tie a
knot.This bookmark fits into a
Pergamano bookmark sleeve
(art.no. 1174).

4 Scarlet Pimpernel

General
The card is made of regular parchment paper and consists of three parts
(card, square and circle). Other material: square of terra cotta coloured
paper.

The Circle

Tracing
Tinta orange (06T): flowers. Tinta
leafgreen (10T): leaves, stems, dots in
flower hearts.

Painting
Tinta orange (06T) and Tinta red
(03T) mixed: flowers. Tinta leafgreen
(10T) and Tinta yellow (16T) mixed:
leaves. Tinta yellow (16T): flower
hearts.

Dorsing (with Dorso-oil)
Dorso Yellow (assort. 1): behind flowers and leaves.

Perforating (shallow)
With 5-needle tool and perforating
tool Semi Circle according to pattern.

Embossing
Flowers, leaves (lightly) and between
Semi Circle perforations.

Perforating (deep)
With perforating tool Semi Circle
again according to pattern. With
5-needle tool (twist left/right) again
according to pattern.

Finishing off
Tinta orange (06T): circles between
5-needle tool perforations. Tinta
leafgreen (10T): lines between
5-needle perforations. Cut out the circle along the Semi Circle perforations.

The Square

Tracing
Tinta white (01T): outline of square,
triangles. Tinta leafgreen (10T): line
inside outline of square.

Embossing
Outlines of triangles and outline of
square. With punch wheel and perforating tool Star according to pattern.
Dots between Star Tool impressions.

Perforating
With 2-needle tool along the inside of
the triangles.

Cutting

Cut out the triangles along the 2-needle perforations.

Finishing off

Emboss along the outside of the square to a depth of 2-3mm and cut out the square using fret-scissors.

The Card

Tracing

Tinta orange (06T): flowers. Tinta leafgreen (10T): leaves, stems, dots in flower hearts. Tinta white (01T): triangles, outline of card.

Painting

Tinta orange (06T) and Tinta red (03T) mixed: flowers. Tinta leafgreen (10T) and Tinta yellow (16T) mixed: leaves. Tinta yellow (16T): flower hearts.

Perforating

With Easy-Grid fine mesh and perforating tool Arrow: triangles according to pattern A.

Embossing

Flowers, leaves, outlines of triangles and outline of card. With punch wheel along outline of card according to pattern.

Finishing off

Fold the card. Perforate along the outline of the card with the 2-needle tool and cut out along these perforations. Glue the parchment square onto the terra cotta tinted square. Cut out the terra cotta tinted square slightly larger than the outline of the parchment square using fret-scissors. Glue the circle onto the square. Glue the square diagonally onto the card. Add a text sticker.

5 Sailing Boats

General

The card is made of regular parchment paper. Other material: red ribbon (20cm long, 3mm wide).

Tracing

Tinta blue (02T): boats, outline of front of card. Tinta red (03T): flags. Tinta white (01T) clouds, sails, birds. Tinta black (11T): picture frame. Tinta leafgreen (10T): coast line.

Painting

Tinta blue (02T): boats, shades is sea (watery). Tinta red (03T): flags. Tinta leafgreen (10T): coast line.

Dorsing (with Dorso-oil)

Dorso orange (assort. 2) + Dorso yellow (assort. 1): sky above clouds. Dorso blue (assort. 1) + Dorso green (assort.2): sea. Dorso blue (assort. 2): parts of clouds.

A

Pattern 4

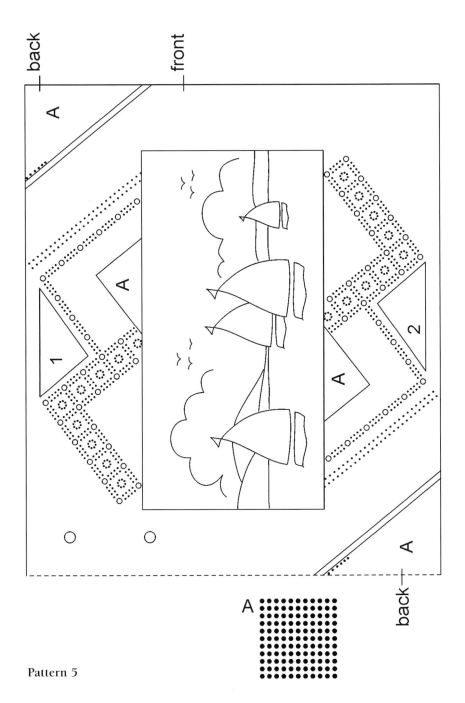

Pattern 5

Perforating (shallow)

With 4-needle tool according to pattern. With Easy-Grid regular mesh and perforating tool Arrow four triangles on front of card and two corners on back of card.

Embossing

Cloud lines, flags, boats, some lines in sea and between 4-needle perforations according to pattern. With embossing tool Hockey Stick: sails. With embossing tool Star according to pattern. With embossing tool Punch Wheel: double dotted lines.

Perforating (deep)

With 4-needle tool again according to pattern.

Cutting

Cut all 4-needle perforations into slits.

Finishing off

Tinta blue (02T): dots in Star Tool impressions. Emboss softly along the straight outline of the card to a depth of 2/3mm. Cut out the front of the card using fret-scissors near the outline of the card. Perforate along the corners of the front of the card with the 2-needle tool and cut them out along these perforations. Make two holes for the ribbon on the front of the card. Thread the ribbon through the holes and tie a knot. Fold the card and cut out the back of the card off straight.

6 Blue Bookmark

General

The bookmark is made of blue Fantasy Parchment 1 (art.no.1599). Other material: blue ribbon (10cm long, 3mm wide).

Tracing

Tinta Pearl blue (02TP): flowers. Tinta Pearl white (01TP): leaves. Tinta gold (22T): wavy lines, outline of bookmark.

Painting

Tinta Pearl blue (02TP): flowers.

Perforating

With Easy-Grid regular mesh and perforating tool Arrow according to pattern A.

Embossing

Flowers, lines in leaves and lines outside the outline of bookmark. With embossing tool Star according to pattern.

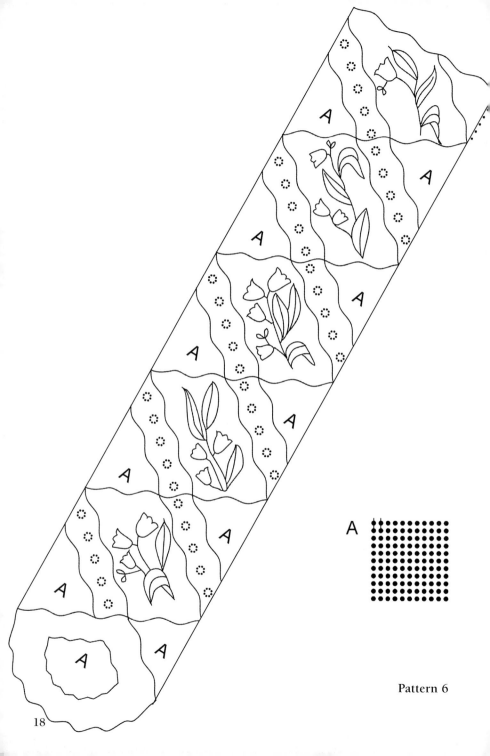

A

Pattern 6

Finishing off
Tinta white (01T): dots in Star Tool impressions. Perforate along the outline of the bookmark with perforating tool 2-Split. Cut out or tear out the bookmark along these perforations. Cut out some Easy-Grid perforations at the bottom, thread the ribbon through the hole and tie a knot. This bookmark fits into a Pergamano bookmark sleeve (art.no. 1174).

7 Thistle in White Work

General
The card is made of regular parchment paper and the inside of card of Parchment Vellum lace (art.no. 1677). Other material: gold ribbon (20cm long, 3mm wide).

Tracing
Tinta white (01T): entire design.

Perforating (shallow)
With 4-needle tool and perforating tool Semi Circle according to pattern. With Easy-Grid regular mesh and perforating tool Diamond according to pattern A.

Embossing
Leaves, thistle heads, along curved outline of card and between 4-needle and Semi Circle perforations according to pattern. With a ruler and 1-needle tool diagonal lines between Easy-Grid perforations.

Perforating (deep)
With 4-needle tool and perforating tool Semi Circle again according to pattern.

Cutting
Cut all 4-needle perforations into slits.

Finishing off
Fold the card. Attach the inside of card with double sided tape inside the card. Perforate along the front and the inside of card with the 2-needle tool and cut out along these perforations. Emboss a line along the outline of the back of the card and cut it off straight. Thread the ribbon through the slits. Add a text sticker.

8 Religious Card

General
The card is made of regular parchment paper. 3-D Elements: cross (of regular parchment paper), two separate fronts of card (one of Parchment Vellum lace (art.no. 1677) and the other one of Parchment Vellum gold (art.no. 1611)).

The Card

Tracing

Tinta white (01T): outline of front of card. Tinta gold (22T): outline of back of card, outline of lace front of card (both according to line A). White pencil: outline of golden front of card according to line B.

Embossing

Along outside of outline of card and lace front of card.

The Cross

Tracing

Tinta violet (07T): violet bells. Tinta yellow (16T): primroses. Tinta leaf-green (10T): leaves, stems. Tinta Pearl white (01TP): bells. Tinta white (01T): curved borderline. Tinta gold (22T): outline of cross.

Painting

PCE 10 and PCE 12 mixed: violet bells. PCE 1: primroses. PCE 15 and PCE 17 mixed: large leaves. PCE 16 and PCE 17 mixed: remaining leaves.

Dorsing (with Dorso-oil)

Dorso light green (assort. 1): flowers and leaves.

Perforating (shallow)

With 4-needle tool according to pattern.

Embossing

Flowers, leaves (lightly), curved borderline, bells, between 4-needle perforations and along outline of cross. With embossing tool Star according to pattern.

Cutting

Cut 4-needle perforations into crosses and slits.

Finishing off

Perforate along the outline of the cross with the 2-needle tool and cut out along these perforations. Fold the card. Perforate along the outline of the card with the 2-needle tool and cut out along these perforations. Cut out the golden front of the card using fret-scissors. Cut the lace front of the card off straight. First glue the cross onto the lace front of the card, then glue the lace front of the card onto the golden front of the card, then glue the golden front of the card onto the front of the card. Keep the bottom of the three parts straight, the card will stand up.

9 Easy Lace card with flowers

General

The card and the insert (on which the flowers are painted) are made of regular parchment paper.

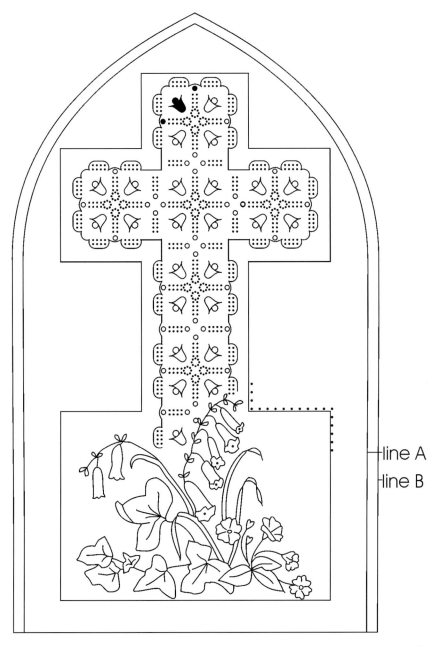

line A

line B

Pattern 8

front

back
insert

Pattern 9

A

Insert

Tracing

Tinta violet (07T): large flowers. Tinta
leafgreen (10T): leaves, stems. Tinta
white (01T): small flowers, outline of
card, corner lines.

Painting

PCE 10 and PCE 12 mixed: large flowers. PCE 1: flower hearts. PCE 16
and PCE 17 mixed: leaves.

Embossing

Small flowers, outline of card and
corner lines. With embossing tool
Hockey Stick: large flowers, leaves.

Lace card

Tracing

Tinta white (01T): outline of card,
scrolls, central panel.

Dorsing (with Dorso-oil)

Dorso violet (assort. 1): front of card,
fading towards centre.

Perforating (shallow)

With 4-needle tool according to
pattern. With perforating tool Four-in-
Four along top and every alternate
row. With Easy-Grid fine mesh and
perforating tool Arrow the scrolls
according to pattern A.

Embossing

Between Four-in-Four perforations,
outline of scrolls and outline of card.

With embossing tool Star according to
pattern. With a ruler and the 1-needle
tool crosses between Four-in-Four
perforations. Emboss on front of card:
centres of semi circles (not the loops).
Leave the central panel at this stage.

Perforating (deep)

With 4-needle tool again according to
pattern. With perforating tool Arrow
(on cutting mat): enlarge the four
holes in centre of Four-in-Four perforations.

Finishing off

Perforate along the inner line of semi
circles with the 2-needle tool and cut
open the perforations inside the semi
circles. Fold the semi circles towards
the front of the card. Emboss the
loops on the back. Perforate along the
scrolls and the central panel and cut
out along these perforations. Keep the
central panel (see TIP at end). Fold
the card. Perforate along the outline
with the 2-needle tool an cut out the
card. Attach with double sided tape
the insert inside the card and the
central panel on the back of the card.

TIP: open the card and lay it flat.
Place the circle directly over the panel
and fix, using removable tape, close to
where the card opens. Place small pie-
ces of double sided tape on the circle.
Fold the back of the card down so
that it sticks to the circle. Carefully
remove the tape whilst the card is
partly closed. Open the card and the

circle is now attached to the back, exactly behind the panel. Use the central panel, which had been cut out, as an area to write on.

10 Happy Anniversary

General
The card and the insert (same size as the square) are made of regular parchment paper. The card has an unusual fold, the square is cut out on two sides and folds across the back. Other material: pink ribbon
(25cm long, 3mm wide).

TIP: photocopy the design on to tracing paper. Attach the back of the tracing paper to the front of the parchment paper. Turn over, emboss on the back of the parchment the double lines of the large hearts, straight double lines. This avoids tracing.

Tracing
Tinta Pearl red (03TP): flowers, outline of card. Tinta gold (22T): leaves. Tinta white (01T): straight double lines. White pencil: outlines of large hearts.

Painting
Pintura Bordeaux (51): flowers. Tinta gold (22T): dots in flower hearts.

Dorsing (with Dorso-oil)
Dorso Magenta (assort. 1): large hearts, along the iside of the outline of card.

Perforating (shallow)
With 4-needle tool and perforating tool Semi Square according to pattern.

Embossing
Straight double lines, double lines of large hearts, line outside the curved outline of card, flowers, leaves and between 4-needle and Semi Square perforations. Emboss on front of card: flower hearts.

Perforating (deep)
With 4-needle tool and perforating tool Semi Square again according to pattern. With perforating tool Arrow (on cutting mat): enlarge the three holes in the heart shapes between Semi Square perforations.

Stippling
With 1-needle tool between double lines of large hearts.

Cutting
Cut 4-needle perforations into crosses according to pattern and between straight double lines into slits. Cut out perforations on two sides of the square.

Finishing off
Perforate along the curved outline of

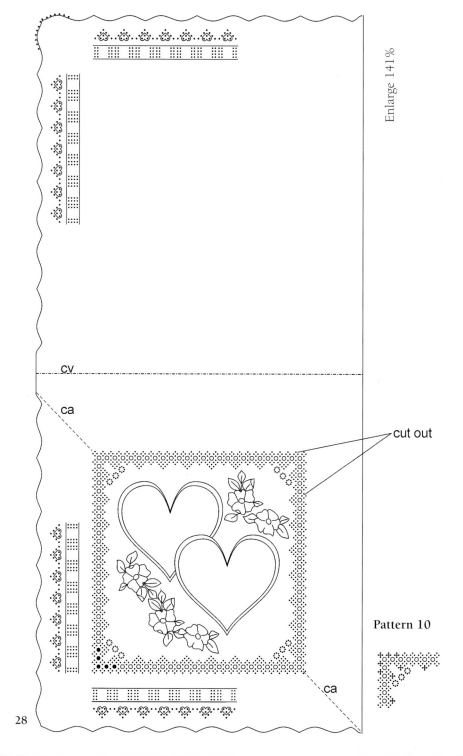

Enlarge 141%

cv

ca

cut out

Pattern 10

ca

28

the card with the 2-needle tool and cut out the card along these perforations. Emboss foldingline CV at the front of the card and the two parts of foldingline CA at the back of the card. Fold the card. Thread the ribbon through the slits. Attach the insert with double sided tape inside the card (see TIP on Easy Lace card pattern). Add a text sticker.

11 Handkerchief card

General
The card is made of regular parchment paper and the insert of Parchment Vellum lace (art.no. 1677). Other material: white ribbon (10 cm long, 3 mm wide).

Tracing
Tinta white (01T): straight lines, outline of card.

Painting (with Perga-Colors Exclusive)
PCE 2, PCE 14, PCE 16: between lines on reverse side.

Dorsing (with Dorso-oil)
Dorso Yellow (assort.1): triangle B.

Perforating (shallow)
With 3-and 4-needle tools and perforating tools Semi Square and Semi Circle according to pattern. With

Easy-Grid regular mesh and perforating tool Arrow: according to pattern A, on back of front of card. With Easy-Grid fine mesh and perforating tool Arrow: along inside of the squares, line in top right corner of back of card.

Embossing
Straight lines, curved lines, heart shapes between Semi Square perforations and around 3-needle perforations. With embossing tool Star according to pattern.

Perforating (deep)
With 4-needle tool and perforating tools Semi Square and Semi Circle again according to pattern. With 3-needle tool (twist left/right) again according to pattern. With perforating tool Arrow (on cutting mat): enlarge the central holes in the heart shapes between Semi Square perforations.

Cutting
Cut all 4-needle perforations into crosses. Cut the Easy-Grid perforations according to pattern.

Finishing off
PCE 14 + PCE 16: dots in Star Tool impressions. PCE 2: dots between 3-needle perforations. Perforate along the curved outlines of front and back of the card with the 2-needle tool. Cut out the card along the 2-needle and the outmost 4-needle perforations.

front back

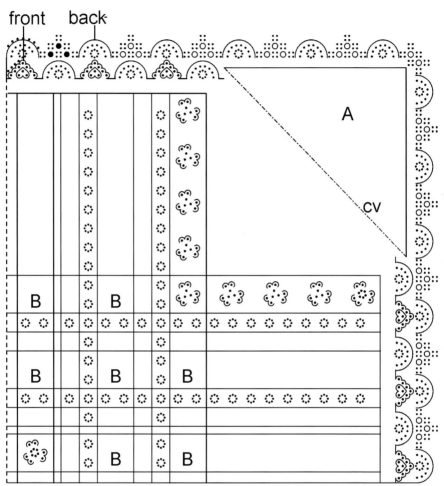

A 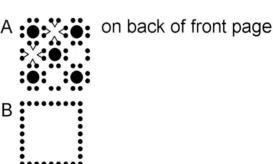 on back of front page

B

Pattern 11

Fold the card and cut the bottom line off straight. Fold the top right corner of the front of the card down and gleu a bow onto the card with a dot of Pergakit. Cut out the the insert using a fancy edge scissors and attach it with double sided tape inside the card. Add a text sticker.

12 Bouquet with Bow

General
The card is made of regular parchment paper and the inside of card of Parchment Vellum lace (art.no. 1677).

Tracing
Tinta Pearl white (01TP): large flowers, hearts, outline of card, text, bow. Tinta turquoise (05T): small flowers. Tinta leafgreen (10T): leaves, stems.

Painting
Tinta Turquoise (05T): small flowers. Tinta leafgreen (10T) and Tinta black (11T) mixed: leaves. Tinta Pearl yellow (16TP): flower hearts, edges of bow. Tinta Pearl sepia (12TP): dots in flowerhearts.

Dorsing (with Dorso-oil)
Dorso yellow (assort. 1): bouquet. Remove any Dorso behind large flowers with an eraser.

Perforating (shallow)
With 4-needle tool and perforating tool Semi Circle according to pattern.

Embossing
Small flowers, leaves, between 4-needle and Semi Square perforations according to pattern and a line outside curved outline of card. Emboss on front of card: large flowers. With embossing tool Hockey Stick: hearts, bow. With embossing tool Star: according to pattern.

Perforating (deep)
With 4-needle tool and perforating tool Semi Circle again according to pattern.

Cutting
Cut out small squares between 4-needle perforations, cut 4-needle perforations into crosses in the outline of card.

Finishing off
Perforate along the curved outline of the card with the 2-needle tool. Cut out the front of the card along the 2-needle, the outmost 4-needle perforations and Semi Circle perforations. Fold the card. Attach the inside of the card with double sided tape inside the card and cut the back of the card and the inside of the card off straight.

Pattern 12

13 Christmas Parcel

General
The card is made of regular parchment paper and the inside of card is made of Parchment Vellum gold (art.no. 1611). 3-D Element: label (of Parchment Vellum gold (art.no. 1611)). Other material: red ribbon (10 cm long, 3mm wide).

The card

Tracing
Tinta gold (22T): outline of card, bells. Tinta Pearl sepia (12TP): stems of fir branches and holly leaves. Tinta sepia (12T): cones. Tinta leafgreen (10T): holly leaves. Tinta red (03T): berries, outline along perforations pattern.

Painting
Tinta sepia (12T): cones, some lines in fir branches. Tinta leafgreen (10T): leaves, some lines in fir branches. Tinta gold (22T): some lines in fir branches. Tintura red (03): berries. Tinta black (11T): dots in berries.

Perforating (shallow)
With perforating tool Semi Star according to pattern. With Easy-Grid fine mesh and perforating tool Arrow: bells according to pattern A.

Embossing
Holly leaves, berries, cones and between Semi Star perforations. With 1-needle tool fine lines in fir branches. With embossing tool Star according to pattern.

Perforating (deep)
With perforating tool Semi Star again according to pattern.

The label

Tracing
Tinta white (01T): outline.

Perforate
With 2-needle tool along outline. With 4-needle tool according to pattern.

Cutting
Cut all 4-needle perforations into slits.

Finishing off
Fold the card. Perforate along the outline of the card with the 2-needle tool and cut out the card along these perforations. Attach the inside of card inside the card. Cut out the inside of card slightly larger than the card using fret-scissors. Thread the ribbon through the slits and glue the label onto the card. Add a text sticker.

14 Snow Scene Christmas Card

General
The card is made of regular parchment paper. Other materials: red ribbon (20cm long, 3mm wide), glitter.

Tracing
Tinta white (01T): cottage, horizon, path, outline front of card. Tinta leafgreen (10T): holly leaves, dots to mark the trees, grass. Tinta gold (22T): bells, outline along scene. Tinta black (11T): fence, chimney, windows, door, text. Tinta red (03T): berries.

Painting
Pintura green (08) and Pintura yellow (16) mixed: leaves, part of trees. Pintura red (03): berries. Tinta black (11T): fence, door, chimney, shades in scene (watery). Tinta gold (22T): windows.

Dorsing (with Dorso-oil)
Dorso black (assort. 2): area above cottage (very softly).

Perforating (shallow)
With 4-needle tool and perforating tool Semi Square according to pattern. With Easy-Grid regular mesh and perforating tool Arrow according to pattern A. On the back of card: with Easy-Grid regular mesh and perforating tool Arrow according to pattern B (first mark with white pencil the curved line as on the edge of front of card).

Embossing
Smoke, holly leaves, berries, scene, between Semi Square perforations and borderline of front of card. With embossing tool Star according to pattern.

Perforating (deep)
With 4-needle tool again according to pattern. With perforating tool Arrow (on cutting mat): enlarge all holes in Semi Square perforations.

Cutting
Cut all 4-needle perforations into slits. Cut out the front of card along the outmost perforations and the back of card along the outmost Easy-Grid perforations.

Finishing off
Fold the card. Thread the ribbon through the slits. Add some glitter on the scene.

15 River Scene

General
The card is made of regular parchment paper.

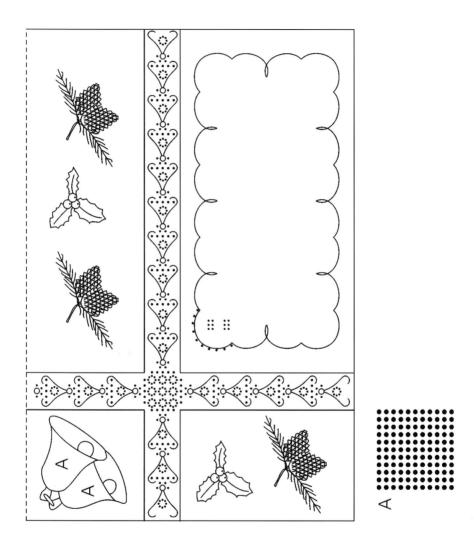

Pattern 13

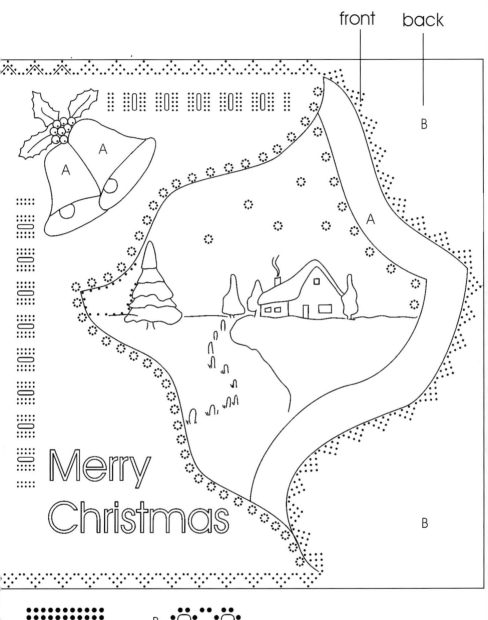

front   back

B

A

A

B

Merry
Christmas

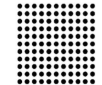

B

Pattern 14

Tracing
Tinta Sepia (12T): boat, houses, river-bank, picket. Tinta leafgreen (10T): leaves, stems, field outlines, line along the inmost line of outline of card. Tinta white (01T): daisies, curved borderline.

Painting (with Perga Colors Exclusive)
PCE 1 + PCE 2: 2 fields, flower hearts, houses. PCE 5 and PCE 8 mixed: tips of petals. PCE 7: top of boat, 2 roof tops. PCE 3: rooftop, riverbank. PCE 13: boat. PCE 15 + PCE 17: leaves. PCE 12 + PCE 14: river. PCE 16 + PCE17: other fields, trees, grass. Tinta leafgreen (10T): small dots in flower hearts.

Dorsing (with Dorso-oil)
Dorso light green (assort. 1): grass, green fields. Dorso yellow ochre (assort. 1) + Dorso yellow (assort. 1): fields, between double lines. Dorso blue (assort. 1) + Dorso magenta (assort. 1): sky.

Perforating (shallow)
With perforating tools Heart-shape and Semi Square according to pattern.

Embossing
Double lines of outline of card, curved borderline, daisies, leaves and between Semi Square perforations according to pattern. With embossing tool Hockey Stick: scene (very lightly). With embossing tool Star between heart shapes perforations.

Perforating (deep)
With perforating tools Heart-shape and Semi Square again according to pattern. With perforating tool Arrow (on cutting mat): enlarge holes within heart shapes in Semi Square perforations and central hole in Heart shaped perforations.

Stippling
With 1-needle tool between double lines of outline of card.

Finishing off
Perforate along the outline of the card with perforating tool 2-Split and cut out or tear out along these perforations. Fold the card and cut the back of the card off straight.

16 Country Scene with 3-D Butterfly

General
The card and the insert are made of regular parchment paper. 3-D Elements: butterfly, extra wing of butterfly (of regular parchment paper).

The Insert

Tracing
With a brush (size 02). PCE 17: grass. PCE 19: houses. PCE 16 + PCE 17: trees, banks. Tinta wit (01T): outline of scene. Tinta yellow (16T): flowers. Tinta gold (22T): double straight lines.

Painting
PCE 16 and PCE 17 mixed: trees, banks. PCE 1: flowers. PCE 3 and PCE 7 mixed: roofs. PCE 11 + PCE 12: river. PCE 3: houses. PCE 14: windows.

Dorsing (with Dorso-oil)
Dorso magenta (assort. 1) + Dorso blue (assort. 1): lines in sky. Dorso light green (assort. 1): behind flowers.

Embossing
Flowers, rest of scene (lightly).

Stippling
With 1-needle tool along border of insert.

The Card

Tracing
Tinta gold (22T): outline of front of card. Tinta yellow (16T): flowers. Tinta leafgreen (10T): leaves, stems. Tinta white (01T): berries, outline of scene, outline of back of card.

Painting
Pinta-Perla yellow (16N) + a little bit of Pintura red (03): petals large flowers. Pinta-Perla yellow (16N): small flowers. PCE 15 and PCE 16 mixed: leaves, flower hearts. Tinta Pearl sepia (12TP): dots in flower hearts.

Dorsing (with Dorso-oil)
Dorso yellow ochre (assort. 1): behind flowers and leaves.

Perforating (shallow)
With 4-needle tool according to pattern.

Embossing
Flowers, leaves, berries, along inside of outline of front of card, outline of scene and between 4-needle perforations. With embossing tool Star according to pattern.

Perforating (deep)
With 4-needle tool again according to pattern.

Cutting
Cut out the central 4-needle perforations into crosses according to pattern.

Butterfly (3-D element)

Tracing
Tinta white (01T): butterfly, extra wing.

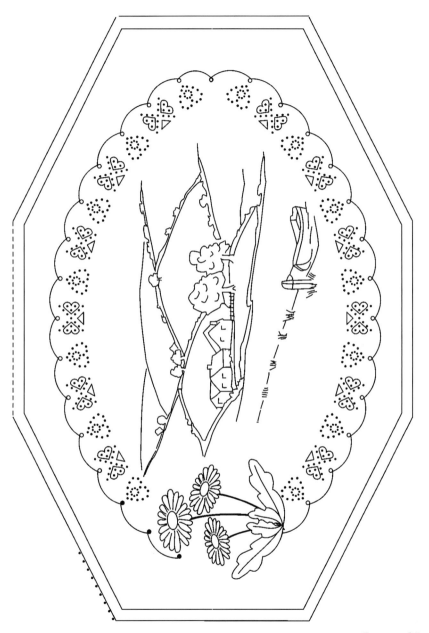

Pattern 15

43

Perforating
With Easy-Grid fine mesh and perforating tool Arrow: parts of wings according to pattern A.

Stippling
With 1-needle tool rest of wings.

Embossing
Body, outlines of wings.

Cutting
Cut out the butterfly and extra wing.

Finishing off
Perforate along the inside of the square with the 2-needle tool and cut out along these perforations. Fold the card. Perforate along the curved outline of the card with the 2-needle tool and cut out along these perforations. Attach the insert with double sided tape inside the card and perforate along the straight outline of the card an the insert with the 2-needle tool and cut out along these perforations. First glue the 3-D element (butterfly) with a little Pergakit onto the card, then glue the extra wing in place.

17 Cockerel

General
The card and the insert (on which the cockerel is painted) are made of regular parchment paper.

The Insert

Tracing
Tinta sepia (12T): beak, eye, feet.

Painting (with Perga-Liners)
In dry technique with parchment paper directly over the pattern: A2, A3, A11, A12, A17, A19, A20: cockerel (make short strokes over the body). With a dampened brush (size 0): brush in the colours in the directions of the feathers. A12: red parts. A18: feet, beak. Tinta leafgreen (10T): grass.

Dorsing (with Dorso-oil)
Dorso yellow ochre (assort. 1): the shape behind the cockerel.

The Card

Tracing
Tinta white (01T): outline of card, central shape. Tinta leafgreen (10T): leaves, stems.

Painting
Tinta leafgreen (10T): leaves.

Dorsing (with Dorso-oil)
Dorso light green (assort. 1): behind leaves.

Perforating (shallow)
With 4-needle tool, perforating tools Semi Square and Flower according to pattern.

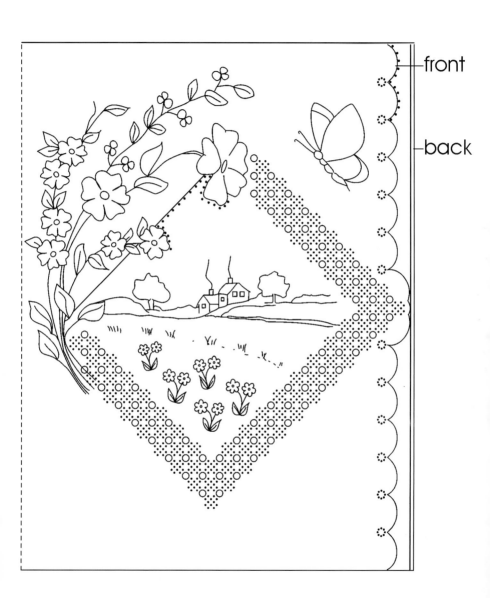

front

back

Pattern 16

Embossing
Between Semi Square perforations, outline of central shape and outline of front of card. With embossing tool Star according to pattern.

Perforating (deep)
With 4-needle tool, perforating tools Semi Square and Flower again according to pattern. With perforating tool Arrow (on cutting mat): enlarge the central holes in the heart shapes in Semi Square perforations.

Cutting
Cut all 4-needle perforations into crosses.

Finishing off
Tinta orange (06T): circles between the Flower Tool perforations in the corner flowers. Perforate along the front of the card and inside the central shape with the 2-needle tool and cut out along these perforations. Fold the card. Attach the insert with double sided tape inside the card. Cut the insert and the back of the card off straight. Add a text sticker.